Designed by Andreea Chiriac

www.ingramcontent.com/pod-product-compliance
Lightning Source LLC
Chambersburg PA
CBHW070425290526
45791CB00005B/1838